Oceans and Orchids

Oceans and Orchids

Poems by

Anne-Marie Derouault

© 2025 Anne-Marie Derouault. All rights reserved.
This material may not be reproduced in any form, published,
reprinted, recorded, performed, broadcast,
rewritten or redistributed without
the explicit permission of Anne-Marie Derouault.
All such actions are strictly prohibited by law.

Cover design by Shay Culligan
Cover image by Maria Louceiro on Unsplash
Author photo by Gregg Zupcsics

ISBN: 978-1-63980-839-7

Kelsay Books
502 South 1040 East, A-119
American Fork, Utah 84003
Kelsaybooks.com

To my mother
whose earthly eyes will not read these lines
but who speaks all languages now

Acknowledgments

Grateful acknowledgments to the editors of the following journals and anthologies, in which some of these poems have previously appeared, sometimes in earlier versions:

Pandemic (Precious Publishing): "Borders Closed, Garden Open" (under the previous title "Borders")

Pen Women online: "Today I Watched the Clouds"

Space Coast Writers Guild Anthologies:
    Horizon: "Places That Shaped Me," "Our Last Shore"
    Survival: "Australian Megafires" (under the previous title "Fires")
    Transformations: "Aging Well," "After a Difficult Week"

U.S. 1 Worksheets Volume 70: "The Stories My Books Tell"

Written in the Sun (Scribblers of Brevard): "And God Created Great Whales" (under the previous title "Marine Creatures"), "My Hour of Peace" (under the previous title "Rain")

My deepest thanks to those who have given me support and inspiration:

The members of the West Windsor Art Council Poetry group, for their critiques and encouragement, especially Anna M. Evans who leads the group with a passion for the many forms of poetry, for her helpful and honest feedback, and for all that I learned from her. Special thanks to my friend Elizabeth Stamper, who introduced me to this inspiring group of poets.

Dorianne Laux, for her vision of poetry and wisdom, and her invitation to dig deep and "write from a lived life."

Christopher (Kit) Adams and Gene Luke, for providing active support and opportunities for writers on the Space Coast.

The Cape Canaveral Branch of the National League of American Pen Women for their warm welcome and encouragements.

Gregg, for his comments and help preparing the manuscript.

The oceans, Nature and her creatures which sustain my inspiration and my awe every day.

Contents

VOYAGES

Places That Shaped Me	15
Parisian Refuge	16
The Stories My Books Tell	17
Sunday Patisserie	18
Seeking Freedom and Other Things in Parisian Bistros	19
Monet's Water Lilies and Japanese Bridge	20
Corsica Mediterranean Night	22
Ocean Pull	24
Our Last Shore	25
When Words Are False Friends	26
The Ocean, the Sky, Driftwood, Shells, Storms, and Florida	27
When the Horizon Gets Hazy	28
Tea Ceremony	30
Today I Watched the Clouds	31
Great Exuma Island	32
In a Perfect World	33
Blue Dome of Greece	34
What Gives You Your Life?	35

PRECIOUS YEARS

A Sailboat Lifted by the Waves	39
How Do You Live Life Well?	40
Self-Portrait—If I Were . . .	42
Things Worth Living For	44
My Hour of Peace	45
Ceramic Cups	46
Ode to a Peaceful Night	47
The Warmth of My Winter	48

In Praise of Dreams	49
Morning Rituals	51
The Purple Threads of My Life	52
A Predestined Encounter	53
Tandava	54
The Last Morning	55
The Land of Absolute Cold	56
When I Am Called	57
All Images Will Disappear	58
A Thousand Names for God	60
Your First Year of Life	61
My Little Prince	62
Aging Well	63

LIVING EARTH

The Healing Stones	67
After a Difficult Week	68
Australian Megafire	69
A Fountain to Walk To	70
Dorian, 2019	71
Borders Closed, Garden Open	72
The Cost of a Poncho Skirt	74
Plea Song	76
And God Created Great Whales	77
At the Edge, a Ghazal	78
Shima	79
I Cannot Touch You	80
Where Are You?	81
Wilderness in My Backyard	82
John James Audubon's Red Feathered Friend	83

FOR MY MOTHER

Encore un Été	87
Birthday in Lockdown	89
14 Things That Made My Days in Normandy	90
Hello From Florida	91
The Colors of Paris 2024	92
That Summer	93
The Great Departure	94
Sixty-Five Years of Our Lives	96
Haikoum for All Hallows Eve	98
Walking My Mother Home	100
Mourning Doves	101
My Mother's Soup	102
Enchanted Episode	103
Your Special Day	104
Aftersense	106
All Will Be Said	107
Heritage	108

VOYAGES

*The true voyagers are those who leave
for the sake of leaving.*
—Charles Baudelaire, *Invitation au voyage*

Places That Shaped Me

Paris came first.
As a little girl I skipped and played
on the grey sidewalks
by my mother's *bijouterie*.

Chestnut trees lined the way to school
the course of their leaves marking the seasons.

As a young woman I discovered South America
in my first month-long trip,
living with close friends in the buzzing city of Caracas,
I learned the sounds of a new language,
spent weekends driving through turquoise shores and green
    grasslands.

The subtle taste of the guavas
the exuberance of the tropics
left a garden in my heart.

After many years and many winters
back in Paris,
on a business trip I landed
in Highland Beach, Florida

and stayed . . .

The ocean washed away the journey.
I drove to work while hibiscuses and orange blossoms
returned the garden to my heart.

Parisian Refuge

A small bistro table against a white wall
receives the Sencha tea in the morning.

    My refuge in the midst of the big city.

I pour a glass of raspberry kefir,
sparkling pink lifts my mood.

    My refuge in the midst of the celebrated city.

A statue of Kwan Yin on the window ledge,
offered by my mother a long time ago.

    My refuge in the midst of the hustling city.

The words of a French poet always around me:
Nature is a book that is always open, the wind turns its pages.[1]

    My refuge in the midst of the thousand-faced city.

Tiny purple flowers and overgrown patches of green
celebrate one more spring.

    In the midst of the vast city
    this place is my refuge.

---

[1] Christian Bobin, *La lumière du monde / The light of the world*

The Stories My Books Tell

Books are the mirrors of the soul.
  —Virginia Woolf

My books are companions that followed me
from adolescence to senior years
from one continent to another.

    L'Etranger by Albert Camus.

Some with yellowed pages and worn covers
others brand new and brightly colored
some studied in depth, others yet unread.

    The Dalai Lama's Cat by David Michie.

Shelf sections once organized
were disturbed through several moves
—psychology with science, spirituality with travel . . .

    The Treasured Writings of Khalil Gibran.

The time has come to lighten
the overflowing shelves
sort through the books along with my life.

    Lying on the Couch by Irvind Yalom.

I will keep the works that shaped me
redistribute the rest,
in the space created,
display a rose quartz and a pearlescent candle.

Sunday Patisserie

>Inspired by Robert Hayden, "Those Winter Sundays"

On the weekdays you brought us handmade bread
from the Parisian bakery where you worked,
crisp golden baguettes and sweet-smelling loaves.
As children we were excited and scared,
fearing your time in bars on the way home,
the sullen mood and angry words
accompanying the blessed gift at times.
How salt and bitter was the bread those days.[2]

On Sundays harmony returned along with your smile
and your promise not to drink again.
You brought us "Opera" pastries
named after the shape of Palais Garnier:
three squares of sponge cake dipped into coffee
filled with butter cream and topped with ganache,
so welcome, and so sweet.

---

[2] Oscar Wilde, "And O how salt and bitter is the bread," in *At Verona*

Seeking Freedom and Other Things in Parisian Bistros

I enjoyed these emblematic places
at every street corner,
offering a respite from the busy city,
alive yet anonymous,
shared yet private.

I used them to study, to write,
in the muted ambiance of the back room.
I used them to read
Krishnamurthi—*Freedom from the known.*
I used them to rest, and dream, and think, and be.

I stayed there to wait,
before an appointment, like a transition,
before a therapy session, to prepare myself.

After two years of pandemic away from Paris,
I looked for a new bistro.
This time I wanted an outdoor terrace not a back room,
with distanced tables and few people, *virus oblige.*
I had a cheddar crêpe with a glass of hard cider.
It tasted like freedom.

Monet's Water Lilies and Japanese Bridge

   Giverny, Normandy

The nympheas surround us.
Reflections of a liquid world,
pink blooms and lush greens
taking root in the silt
rising to the light.

A meditative space of pastel and peace
as the artist intended.
A garden and a pond he created
so he could live and paint
nature again and again,
changing with the weather, the time of day, the plants.
What I need most are flowers, he said.

Hundreds of variations ended up
in Paris, Washington, New York, Princeton . . .
One immense canvas was given to France
on November 11, 1918,
in celebration of the armistice.

You and I walked that bridge,
you took many pictures
of the rose garden, the water lilies,
the pond and the house.
We followed the painter's steps
silently, joyfully.

Unaware of your own bridge to cross,
sometime soon.

Corsica Mediterranean Night

A night like any night,
unforgettable yet magical.
A window opening to the darkness,
her Majesty the moon was playing with the clouds,
full, round and white, a sign of infinity.

> The bed faces this *théâtre vivant*.
> We are inside the tableau.
> Your skin is tanned and I don't know you.
> Two bodies lying still on the white sheets,
> bathed with light. Dazzled by the stars.
> Holding hands when the moon is hidden,
> lovers when the moon reappears.
> In between, a space with no word,
> no time and no self-consciousness.
>
> Are we uniting with Her?
> Are we uniting with ourselves?
> I am the Moon and you are the Sun.
> The embrace is stronger than we are,
> in the eternal play of energies
> coming together and apart
> in rhythm with life and death.

How many lovers throughout the world,
at that moment,
are finding each other and then
pulling away?
The same lifeforce pulsates above the sea,
I hear it in our blended breath,
in our voices, in our touch.
Words not spoken die on our lips.

We were lonely children,
wounded animals, forgetful gods.

Ocean Pull

Ocean lights me up.
Glistening blue in the Mediterranean,
turquoise in tropical waters,
its ever-changing colors play with the sun,
its waves are liquid light.

Ocean is my magnet.
It guides my travels, shapes all my escapes
—Greek Santorini, a Caribbean ashram, Channel island sailing—
for a glimpse, a moment of awe.
It defines my journey across continents,
to make my home along its shore
and live in its presence.

Ultramarine in the Atlantic depth,
steel blue in the Northern seas,
its beaches are an invitation,
its view an exhilaration.
Ocean lights me up.

Our Last Shore

Stunned. Alive.
Mediterranean dazzling,

white house by the sea,
I have arrived.

Blue vibrations enter
body and soul.

Crowds, dusty air, hours in the plane,
crossing the Atlantic, forgotten.

I need kombucha, tea,
to tolerate such beauty

in the company of your paintings,
where you are not.

The house that you found,
the grilled fish at sunset.

Walking that long stretch of beach
to the lighthouse,

where the village ends
where our story ended

until next time
on the other plane.

When Words Are False Friends

Eventually / Eventuellement

Some words changed their meanings
as the waves carried them
across the ocean
from European lands
to American shores.

Eventually I changed too,
during my journey
from continent to continent,
from the grey sidewalks
by my mother's jewelry shop
to the lush red hibiscus
on my way to work.

Sometimes I still use the word
in its original meaning
éventuellement
—possibly, potentially.

I like to leave the door open
for different futures.
I like to allow
for a range of possibilities
and a degree of freedom.

Eventuellement I will return.
But maybe not.

The Ocean, the Sky, Driftwood, Shells, Storms, and Florida

You say, what about the summer heat,
the unescapable fire of the sun,
the blazing light?

Yes but . . . the new meaning of Fall,
the sweetness of "November",
the glowing hibiscuses, the fragrant plumerias
—year around.

You say, what about unexpected storms,
the dangers of winds stronger than us,
roofs flying, houses crumbling?

Yes but . . . the refreshing breeze at night,
the gifts carried to shore
—shells, ancient driftwood,
the radiant skies.

You say, what about the floods,
the dangers of rising waters,
the wake of destruction?

Yes but . . . the ocean,
the expansive horizon of ever-changing blues,
the sound of tropical rain,
dolphins playing in the rivers.

It's where I belong.

When the Horizon Gets Hazy

Tomorrow, at dawn, when the countryside turns pale, I will leave.
—Victor Hugo

I will go, carried by the light,
lifted by the sea,
drawn to a white house
on the south shore of Andalusia.

I will walk on the silver sand
of the endless beach
at the foot of the Sierra Almijara.

Protected from view
by oleanders and bougainvilleas
on the lush terrace,
alone at last,
I will have no plan,
no obligation.

I will drive along the coastal road,
and I will only see the liquid sapphire.

When the horizon gets hazy
from the blurred blue of sea and sky
I will forget
what I need to forget.

During a piece of eternity,
I will be there.
And even when I am gone
I will still be there.

Tea Ceremony

I am in love with green tea,
its names, evocative of exotic countries.

> The names, evocative of exotic countries,
> form a song in my head.

A soft song in my head
—*sencha midori, long jing, makaibari.*

> *Sencha midori, long jing, makaibari,*
> the names are a journey.

Green tea starts my daily journey
while the news waits, while the emails wait.

> While the notifications wait, while the world waits,
> it tastes like grass, like flowers, like dreams.

It tastes like earth, like wood, like dreams.
I am in love with green tea.

Today I Watched the Clouds

> Inspired by an interview with JMG Le Clezio,
> 2008 Nobel Prize in Literature

Today I watched the clouds.

What serendipity
found me lying down
in the middle of a lawn?
Heart filled by the trees' deep green,
social temptations put aside,
my gaze fell into the sky
and got lost.

A few clouds follow their course,
very slow, very light, and very sure.
Le Clezio could see a whole world
in their infinite nuances of white,
of velvety grey,
their unraveling delicate edges,
their cotton candy texture.

Forever tranquil and strong,
they glide into the summer air,
and I glide with them,
serene and destined,
absorbing their suspended peace,
surrendering to their floating journey,
becoming their liquid freedom.

Great Exuma Island

An island chain in the Caribbean,
one cay for each day of the year,
most of them uninhabited.
Orchids and bromeliads,
blow holes and lagoons.
Exuberant.

A veranda by the shoreline,
both in the world, and away from it.
Eyes lost in the changing turquoise,
an emotion comes, an impression,
that all will be well.
Exalted.

Later, immersed in the crystal waters,
flowing with the parrotfish,
the anemones and seagrasses,
hearing the silence
of an underwater world.
Exhaling.

In a Perfect World

Air is sparkling,
breathed into life,
crisp in the early
dawn, charged with *prana*.
Earth is moist,
filled with vegetation,
ground undulating across
hills and valleys,
islands and coastal towns.
Joyful birds wear all
kinds of colors, blue, gray and pink, singing
liquid notes or loud calls.
Mountains defy the sky,
never fully mastered.
Oceans spread far and wide,
Pacific blue and salty Red sea.
Quiet lakes and raging rivers leave
shells and stones along the way,
trees line their banks. The
universe expands,
vast and limitless into
waves of sound and light,
x-rays of space, inviting us to
yield to our curiosity and
zoom into the infinite.

Blue Dome of Greece

Nikos Rigopoulos took some of the most famous pictures
of the village of Oia
at the northwest tip of Santorini Island.

Fascinated by the views,
crowds of tourists, artists and writers
have come to bask in the infallible sun
shining on the whitewashed houses
gleaming above the Mediterranean waves.

We were once fascinated too.
We climbed three hundred steps
on the back of a mule,
we slept on a pebble beach,
our skin salty, our life ahead of us.

The picture has kept me company,
—light during days of winter,
—cerulean blue inside dark buildings,
reminder of an alive space inside me.

It had to be on the cover of my first book,
today a print is on my office wall
on the shore of another ocean.
Greece is there, and hope is there

because I can always go back.

What Gives You Your Life?

Blue roofs of Santorini above the sea,
whitewashed houses, now hanging on my wall,
the Mediterranean light appeases my heart.

The flame of a candle flickers and soothes the mind.
"What gives you your life?" asks Christian Bobin.

Oceans, words, wild flowers, the company of trees,
the little hand of my nephew, my mother's green eyes,
traveling my two countries.

Brought back from India, a sandalwood paperknife
to cut open the pages of a handmade book.
At dusk, a glass of Samos dessert wine.

PRECIOUS YEARS

*Tell me, what is it you plan to do
with your one wild and precious life?*
—Mary Oliver, *The Summer Day*

A Sailboat Lifted by the Waves

You know who I am
  —Leonard Cohen

I am the way I am,
drawn to the silence of the written word,
away from the loud voices
of my childhood,
a sailboat lifted by the waves.

I am the way I am,
a nature lover
shaped by the sand of Atlantic beaches,
the summer months in a rented white house,
a sailboat lifted by the waves.

Yet I know I am deeper than the ways I am,
intrigued by the unseen
since that palm reading when I was ten,
attracted by the quiet beneath the world,
a sailboat lifted by the waves.

How Do You Live Life Well?

Travel to see the world
—walking lighthearted
in the streets of the cities I love,
Malaga, Pondicherry, Paris.

Work to create something new
—a technology to make machines
understand human voices,
helping many, like my mother.

Love and unite
—with nature, ocean, mountains and fields.
Love and connect
—with friends, clients, children and cats.

Enjoy and play
—with the earth, with flowers,
with pens, with books
with fruits, with greens.

Grow and ripen
—work on fear and guilt
to reveal the light
and find freedom.

Do nothing,
breath breathes itself.
Listen to the sound of the universe,
be.

Self-Portrait—If I Were . . .

If I were an animal,
I would be an antelope
running free in the depth of a forest.
If I were a plant,
I would be an ancient olive tree
with branches reaching for peace.

If I were a place,
it would be anywhere outdoors
because it brings me inward.
If I were a city,
it would be Nice with its paved streets
overlooking the sea.

If I were a song, it would be
"Bird on a Wire" by Leonard Cohen.
I have tried, in my way, to be free.
If I were a book, it would be
"The Atlantic Man" by Marguerite Duras.
You and the sea, you are but one for me.

If I were a drink,
it would be green tea,
sweet and strong.
If I were a dish,
it would be a mushroom quiche,
warm and savory.

If I were a season
it would be summer.
If I were a time of day
it would be mid-morning.

If I were a day in my life,
it would be today.

Things Worth Living For

The sight of big oak trees, rooted in the earth, reaching up to the sky.

The sound of human voices, soft and melodious like my friend Jyoti's.

The texture of cat fur, the touch of my nephew's hand.

The smell of freshly cut grass, the fragrance of white gardenias.

The taste of warm buttered scones, the savor of a twenty-year-old Port.

White houses and cobblestone streets, calling for a stroll.

The seven seas and their expansive horizons.

Summer and its extravagance, clear mornings and their promise.

Silence, where everything returns.

My Hour of Peace

Rain fills the air this morning,
falling on the cypress trees,
shining on the smooth lawn,
sounding on the roof.

Droplets of light,
liquid diamonds gliding
down the patio screen,
soft sounds surround me,
a call back to elemental existence.

The instant is suspended,
no obligation,
life is slow and sweet.
The soul touches down,
drops her burdens, and rests.

I drink my Sencha green tea,
Earth drinks the water of life.

Ceramic Cups

> Wabi Sabi: beauty in imperfection and simplicity

Smooth and bright,
artistically painted
—cherry blossoms, blue waves, animal prints or city views
souvenirs of joyous trips,
ceramic cups share our days.
Solitary morning tea,
coffee with friends,
calming night drink.

Nestled in our hands,
they whisper words of courage when days are tough,
they rejoice in our quiet moments.
In a culture of disposables,
they last for ages,
flawed yet enduring vessels for all that comes.

Ode to a Peaceful Night

An unbroken night,
journey through the wildest dreams.

Deep night where the self disappears
allowing the heart to travel

and return inspired,
strengthened and kind.

Night of repair
night of forgiveness

night of healing
night of forgetting.

While the body rests
the mind gathers

for an extraordinary morning
where everything seems possible.

The Warmth of My Winter

This is how I survive winter.
Ayurvedic oil warms my bones,

      sandalwood and sesame warm my bones.
      Miso soup strengthens my body.

The hearty soup sustains my body
with its salty, oceanic flavors,

      with its dried seaweed flavor,
      like umami rich green tea.

Drinking the Gyokuro green tea
in the silence of a winter garden,

      I contemplate the silent garden,
      wrapped in a padded purple coat.

The furry hood of a padded purple coat,
that's how I survive winter.

In Praise of Dreams

Dreams are flights of the soul
              —Robert Moss

In my dreams
I see people,
unknown guides,
or aspects of myself,
I try to understand
their messages.

With a young man on an island,
we're watching the raging seas
we need to cross to reach the land.
He says, how about a taxi instead?
—Alternatives.

Trivial dreams, epic dreams,
infinite landscapes
of oceans and meadows,
limitless body
flying high or free falling.

A sailboat at night on the Mediterranean,
I'm sitting on the deck staring at the water,
lost in the full moon.
—Reflection.

In my dreams
I see people
passed on years ago,

unexpected visits
from my invisible tribe.

My father is back.
He sits at the lunch table with us.
No trace of anger, no trace of alcohol.
—Reconciliation.

Morning Rituals

Splash my face
with cold water,
dissipate the night,
embrace wakefulness.

Prepare my tea,
inhale its green fragrance,
a promise to renew
my desire to live.

Sit by the trees
look at the sky
listen to mantras
watch my cat.

Write in my journal
remember my dreams
set an intention for the day
hug my companion.

When I am ready,
turn on my phone,
read the news,
connect to the world affairs.

Stretch, walk, meditate.
Live this day.

The Purple Threads of My Life

Handmade in crochet, my first shawl was purple,
gifted by a Breton woman when I was twelve.

I covered the wall of my student room
with an Indian print, in mauve.

In Provence I walked the fields of lavender,
always picked a bouquet for my mother.

Amethyst reflections of Mediterranean sunsets
filled the horizon and captured my eyes.

A mix of calming blue and fiery red,
—my violet dress, plum blanket, lilac pen.

A Predestined Encounter

First thing I noticed that night,
your eyes, blue like the waves.

You came to find me, the moon was bright,
your gaze drew me in like a cave.

You guided the boat on the Caribbean Sea
to the retreat center nested in the palm trees.

I was lost, but at that moment I found
a bond so strong it would heal the wounds.

Although we had never met, I recognized you.
You said you had seen me in a dream before.

For hours, astounded, I watched the shore
voiceless, pondering—can this be true?

Then I made friends with the very sky above.
I became invulnerable when I fell in love.

Tandava

A dance of creation, destruction, and release

Music was playing, slow and soft,
I started to dance.
I let the air hold me,
breath moving freely
body flowing like a sea plant.

I surrendered the sorrow,
the hopes, the illusions,
the time wasted,
the failed attempts to reach you
when you could not see me.

Stranger I came,
stranger I went.
I will dance and walk and run and swim
to my soul's content,
to calm the water of thoughts.
Our unborn story will leave
a tiny ripple.

The Last Morning

That morning when I found you,
you were there and you were not.
Wide open blue eyes looking into something
I could not see.
Perhaps the great light that called you once before,
the absolute light of love you said.
You were not afraid.
I felt your calm face, smooth and cold.

You must have glided into peace
like into warm nurturing water.
You must have walked through the stone wall
to the garden you loved.
You must have enjoyed the space and the rising sun.
You must have felt weightless and free.

A few hours after your leaving,
the orchid in your room opened her long-awaited buds
—deep red core and pale-yellow petals.
—a gift.

The Land of Absolute Cold

You came in a dream yesterday . . .
I saw you walking through icy fields
and snow-covered forests, past ancient castles,
at ease and free.
I wanted to join you.
I reached and reached and called your name.
In vain.
Shouldn't lovers travel together?

I woke up and remembered
that last month your soul sailed away,
and how later that French morning,
the orchid you cared for bloomed,
unexpected and bright yellow
against the frost.

When I Am Called

I hope to see the dazzling light
that you once described.
I hope to enter the tunnel,
like a long passage
into unknown territory
and join you.

When we are finally home,
delivered from the tricky pursuits,
having returned all our badges,
unstuck at last,
we will glide above
cities and oceans,
wildflowers and stadiums.

Death on earth made gentler by a tunnel of light.

All Images Will Disappear

> Inspired by Annie Ernaux, Nobel prize of literature 2022,
> and her appearance at "La Grande Librairie" show.

Today I met you, an 82-year-old grande dame.

You speak about being a defector,
having become a professor
after growing up in the working part of town,
never sure if you were legitimate.
And I wonder if I betrayed my own class too.

At some point you recite a passage
strong, crude at times, real, poignant,
from your book *Les Années—The Years*.

All images will disappear, you say,
behind the foreheads of the dead,
gardens behind stone walls, children at play,
young men at war, young women abused . . .
They will live on for a while in the memory of others,
one day the generations will be replaced,
and memories will be lost.

My own images flash before my eyes.
In the next few days
I pay attention, consciously gathering
the images of my life.

Sitting on a bench by the ocean,
watching the equinox tide with my mother.
The joy of my beloved nephew with a new toy,
walking through the forest, his little hand in mine.
The rolling landscapes of Normandy,
villages with more cows than inhabitants.

The images will disappear,
yet we have to live as if,
and continue to write as if, they won't.

Write life—*écrire la vie,* as you say.

A Thousand Names for God

Where is it written
that "God" would
stop wars, fires, diseases?
God, my dear, is as simple as the sun,[3]
says the poet.

The still and silent
background of existence.

When it gets really quiet
and I close my eyes,
I hear it—the liquid sound
of a shell onshore.

A thousand forms of God,
one essence,
atoms and galaxies
newborns and elders

briar and roses.

---

[3] Christian Bobin

Your First Year of Life

> *The odds are we should never have been born.*
> —Dorianne Laux, *Life on Earth*

Your precious life is one-year old today.
One year, since you gave us the delight
of joining us on the blue planet.
One year since you had the good fortune
to be born, in the heart of the Loire valley
amongst hundred-year-old trees and golden buttercups.

We watched you smile at a wooden rattle
—and we smiled.
We followed your discovery of a crib mobile
—and we saw the world afresh.
We read the wonder on your face for a stone, for a leaf
—and we were reminded of humble marvels.

You will not remember
this one blue candle
on a homemade cake.
But while your face is fashioned
from the vestiges of your innocence,
many more candles will come.

My Little Prince

What is essential is invisible to the eye.
—Antoine de Saint-Exupéry, *The Little Prince*

Holding your little hand in mine,
as we walk along Ocean Boulevard,
in the coastal village of Pornichet,
suddenly the figures appear.

Bright and colorful,
—horses, chariots, boats, planes
straight out of Jules Verne,
an old-fashioned merry-go-round.

You choose the submarine, twice.
Later I listen to your magical adventures
on the wooden carousel.
And for a moment I see, too,

as the Zen master says,
a world unseen since childhood.[4]

---

[4] John Greer

Aging Well

First she chooses her cup
—light blue with a golden thread,
or an image of Buddha painted on it.

She draws the bright metallic box out of the cabinet,
delicately opens it to avoid any spill,
smells the aroma in anticipation. A promise.
She lets the tea infuse twice longer than recommended.

The first cup is strong with a bite.
She feels the jolt of energy running
from her tongue down her spine. Multiple flavors combine.
A bouquet of sensations to discover.

The second cup, brewed from the same green leaves,
brings new hidden aromas. Softer, calmer, deeper.
A luxury to experience.

The third cup is an offering from the lavish leaves.
The taste is now lighter, sweeter, and familiar.
An extended gift to sip and savor.

Then she cleanses her cup
so it may be used again and again.

LIVING EARTH

The earth is my witness.
—Gautama Buddha

The Healing Stones

During your teenage years
when asked about wishes for birthday or Christmas
your answer was always the same:
stones, to add to your collection.

    A geode from Mexico with purple amethyst inside.

Every trip I took
I looked for new crystals for the niece I loved.
Over the years your collection grew,
elegantly displayed on the wall.

    Green veined malachite from Africa.

You started to study the healing properties
of these special rocks:
protection, grounding, calm, concentration.

    Bright yellow citrine from Brazil.

You went on to live in a "tiny house"
off the grid amongst the trees,
taken care of by the earth, the sun and the groundwater.

    Blue green fluorites from Colorado.

A young Ukrainian boy now lives in your room.
Every night he touches the stones.
His favorite is the yellow citrine:
vitality and new beginnings.

After a Difficult Week

I open a window to the morning sky,
—infinite blue space.

Pearly clouds floating in the blue space
drift with the breeze.

I welcome the soft breeze,
air in, dust out.

Dust, thoughts, and poisons out.
I breathe in.

I breathe the light in
sun in, shadows out.

Shadows and sorrows out,
a chance to begin again.

To begin again a better day,
I open a window to the morning sky.

Australian Megafire

Some say the world will end in fire.
—Robert Frost

It's Hell on Earth.
Creatures fleeing everywhere.
The flames burn so far and so fast
no one can put them out.

Is it the end of the world
in which we could ignore
the changes to come?
In which we could continue to believe
in infinite abundance
and unlimited resources . . .
Is this where a cycle ends?

Will we know how to reinvent
ways to live
in harmony with our space,
in harmony with our planet?

We need to help her heal,
regreen the burnt grounds
in a few dozen years,
save what can be saved,
and work towards some kind
of Paradise on Earth.

A Fountain to Walk To

*To the salesclerk who sold pills invented to quench thirst:
if I had fifty-three minutes to spend as I liked, the Little Prince
said, I'd walk very slowly toward a water fountain . . .*
—Antoine de Saint-Exupéry

Broken and put away for years,
our water fountain found a new life
by the front door.
Clear water flowing again
which brings renewed energy and harmony,
according to ancient Feng-Shui.

Eight streams cascade down
two levels of large bowls,
smooth and alabaster white.
They produce a serene sound,
regular and undisturbed,
clearing the mind every time I pass by.

The sound echoes its big sister in Rome,
the Fountain of the Four Rivers I once admired,
where people used to carry water home,
where today's crowds enjoy
a magical atmosphere at night.

I like to think that our own fountain
provides water for birds and other creatures.
I like to hear the peaceful sound
and be reminded
to   walk   slowly.

Dorian, 2019

I came for the ocean, the sand and the heat,
filled with the wonder of Florida plumerias,
over a hundred kinds of palm trees,
and everlasting summers.
Never heard the word "hurricane."

Hurricanes, shaped in the eternal spiral
at the core of our cells.
Sometimes we pray to them,
in a desperate attempt to influence their course.
We prayed to Dorian.

Many summers later,
with all the protections available,
—shutters, generators, metal roof,
I still feel so fragile,
so exposed.

We give them names to keep them at a distance.

Borders Closed, Garden Open

Surviving the Great Isolation, March 2020

Tears came
while reading the announcement yesterday,
late evening . . . again . . . too late
of course.

We're living in extraordinary times.
Borders closed,
no more flights to connect my two countries
for at least thirty days.
Unheard of
in twenty years of Florida living.

That day when the world woke up
split into several continents, suddenly
separate and disconnected.

We will survive.
For now, take care of myself,
curl up on the beach,
listen to sacred chants,
calm and collected.
Stay home.

Fortunately there is a garden,
which saved me before
and will save me again,
water for swimming,
relaxing the body,
big trees.
One can hold out for a long time
in the company of trees.

I carry the image of a Mediterranean cove
deep within.
Call on it often.

The Cost of a Poncho Skirt

My hippie-style poncho,
vintage from the late seventies,
kept me warm for many years.
Coverall for cold nights around a bonfire,
or long skirt with fringes and pointing patterns
for dancing parties.

A gift from my sister,
made of llama wool,
—brown, beige, and black rough fibers.
Carrying the ambiance of the Andes mountains
where the llamas live above ten thousand feet.
Handknitted by Peruvian women,
sold on colorful open-air markets
to European merchants.
Finally arriving
in a trendy boutique along Boulevard Saint Michel
in the Latin Quarter where students live and shop.

I enjoyed its uniqueness,
its relaxed fashionable shape,
the easy comfort it provided,
the remnant of the yarn's earthy scent.

I did not know
it takes two years
for the llama's coat to regrow
after the shearing
—two cold winters.

I did not know
the llamas are tied down,
often cut and stitched up
after the shearing,
even pregnant mothers.

Plea Song

> After Lucille Clifton's Sorrow Song

for the eyes of the creatures,
when they suffer,
when they die,
for the transfixed
eyes of the animals, overwhelmed,
the lost eyes of the dolphins swimming in circles,
the eyes of the llamas in the Andes,
stitched up and freezing after the shearing,
the eyes of the cows crying for days
after their missing calf,
for the terrified eyes of the cashmere goats in Asia,
the eyes of the skinned white foxes in the Arctic,
for the eyes of the male chicks alive in the grinder,
the eyes of the drugged horses waiting to die
on the side of the race track,
for all we know, for all we don't know,
for their eyes staring at us,
horrified to see
the mindless ignorance
in mindful people.

And God Created Great Whales

A symphonic poem for orchestra and recorded whale sounds
by Alan Hovhaness

We came a long way for a chance to see you
leaving for a while the comfort of our land
to meet the Great North
and the icy oceans
where you play
majestic and free.

And you came,
to the untold appointment
to grant us the invaluable gift
of moving before our eyes.
How grace can unite
with such a massive body
remains a mystery.

My mind cannot comprehend
the measure of your weight, forty tons . . .
Forty tons of pure animal energy
of primordial force of Yin
great, black and flowing.

Time stands still while I watch you,
for having seen your splendor
and for belonging
to the same universe.

At the Edge, a Ghazal

Baby turtles are born in the sand by the ocean
then run to save their lives, into the ocean.

When I was a young girl I sailed with wonder
along the rocky shores of the Atlantic Ocean.

On Sunday we go to worship with the sandpipers,
commune with the fragrance and the foam from the ocean.

My nephew likes to play with his brand-new bucket
and tries endlessly to empty the ocean.

The waves of the thoughts slow down and rest
on the meditation bench,—*silence is an ocean.*[5]

When we walk in step, we laugh, or we really talk,
when we drop the masks, there is an openness—like an ocean.

If Anne-Marie could choose where to die one day,
she would wait quietly at the edge, at the edge of the ocean.

---

[5] *Silence is an ocean. Speech is a river.* —Rumi

Shima

>A Hopi word meaning "love"

Your death is a month old
and I still can't look at your pictures.

I recall the warmth of your fur
as you breathed your last,

your little body wrapped in a purple blanket,
your lifeless eyes after the injection.

I kept putting words on the page,
but for weeks I could not write.

I travel with your pictures
in case I need to remember,

you curled up on my yoga mat,
jumping on top of my car,

settling on my keyboard,
sleeping in the garden.

The sensation of your fur
left its imprint on my hand.

I will touch you through all creatures,
forever.

I Cannot Touch You

A tourist town
you're strolling alongside a restaurant building
I follow you
trying to stroke you
to protect you.
You're so small
miniature tiger
someone could step on you.
You slip through a door ajar
you find the kitchen.
Before I can catch you
you select a space
in a picture on a wall.
You enter the tableau
I hold it on my heart.

Thank you for coming into my dream.

Where Are You?

Are you in the red wooden box on the memorial table,
in the white fur clipped for us to save,
in the paw print on the alabaster heart shape,
or the collage on my wall showing moments of your life?

Are you on your favorite chair, fascinated by the pool,
on the outdoor cabinet, following the squirrels play,
are you on the couch with us watching TV,
are you in the warmth of the linen sheets against my skin?

On the anniversary of your departing,
I bring to my ear the conch shell we found
on the beach that day, a rare shell.
I hear its sound, a purr like yours.

The space you opened in my heart
eighteen years ago
glows with golden light,

that's where you are.

Wilderness in My Backyard

    A duplex

He came, wild and free,
        a young lynx in our backyard.

His spotted brown fur in the backyard,
        walking   slowly   besides the tall cypresses.

The silhouettes of the cypresses
        surreal in the fog bathed morning.

A birdsong ballet in the early morning,
        robins, sparrows, filled the silence.

I watched him in awe and silence,
        saw his mother following not long after.

Not long after,
        the sun dissipated the fog.

The sun has evaporated the fog.
        When can I be wild and free?

John James Audubon's Red Feathered Friend

When he's here in the morning,
crimson attracting the eyes,
his presence a small miracle,
his song brightens up the garden.

When he's here in the morning,
it's a good sign. The day begins
with beauty and bonding.
We are friends from afar.

I watch him, looking at nothing else.
I love him, without possession, without control
over when he lands or flies away.

And that makes us both free.

FOR MY MOTHER

My mother raised me, and then freed me.
—Maya Angelou, *Even the Stars Look Lonesome*

Encore un Été

July 2021

While you were seeking your breath,
we were holding ours,
calling air and light on you,
surrendering to the precious healing oxygen,
to your lifeforce.

To your angels . . .
The ones above that were watching over you,
protecting you from afar
with a series of coincidences:
right people at the right time,
a room suddenly available,
tall trees through the window,
a white statue of Mary,
a parking spot by the entrance.

With a few bruises
to your soul and your body,
with and despite all this,
you are going to get out!
You are doing well,
forever grateful
to science and the vaccine
which softened the ailment,
and a dedicated, thorough team.

You are going to get out!
We will go to the countryside,

rebuild our health,
be together,
welcome the young new life
your great granddaughter,
who was coming into the world
while you were fighting.
Soak in the sun,
enjoy the garden,
see the ocean.

See the ocean . . .

Birthday in Lockdown

May 16, 2020

For you who know
the softness of a pear
the green shades of spring through the open window
the bitter taste of tea and the sweet one of port,

for you who hear
the beloved voices
sometimes joyful
sometimes serious
through the screen in your palm,

for you who enjoy
your great grandchild growing—on Facebook
his funny faces
his irresistible laughter
the touch of the wool and the clothes you knit for him
—bright colors and many shapes—

life becomes simple and slow,
connected still.
Here are a few paper kisses
across the ocean

for you.

14 Things That Made My Days in Normandy

Wearing my purple puffer coat for the first time,
surviving freezing Paris weather.

Shopping for fabrics with my sister,
bursting into laughter for no reason.

Seeing a jackrabbit in the field next door,
watching the wonder on my nephew's face.

Being moved by a Poetic Resistance reading [6],
getting a warm hug from an unknown young girl.

Eating lunch at an outdoor café,
rebuilding the world with a friend.

Walking around a Breton port under the rain,
having a crêpe with a glass of hard cider.

Finally getting my mother out of the hospital,
taking her to the ocean.

---

[6] *Résistance Poétique* by Cyril Dion

Hello From Florida

Dear Mom,

I am back here for a short while.

Weather is warm of course,
I wear the dress you gave me.
The wall in my office wears a picture of you.

Yesterday I walked the beach.
I watched the sandpipers facing
into the wind, and the waves
washing ashore sculpted pieces of wood.

Last weekend we sailed on the Blue Cypress Lake
and waited to see ospreys feed their young.

The wall in my office wears a picture of you.

The Colors of Paris 2024

The earth is blue like an orange
       —Paul Eluard

Red, the stripes on workers' jackets
putting up barriers along the Champ de Mars,
my childhood playground,
forty-two days before the Olympics.

Gray, the sidewalks
blurred with crowds of tourists,
the prefab buildings next to the Eiffel tower,
the cloud cover and even the car I rented.

Green, the lime trees surrounding the Tilleuls square,
the Seine river lined with outdoor shops
selling 1900s postcards,
the fragrant jasmine climbing my mother's window.

Blue, the glimpses of sunny sky,
the hydrangea blooms at the Tourville café terrace,
the shawl she wears every day,
her eyes when she laughs.

That Summer

    July 2024

We will remember everything.

Children drawing heart shaped flowers for you
afternoons in the park watching them play
my brother driving us to the ocean
despite the light rain
the promenade along the boulevard
in a typical Breton village
my sister's friendly spacious house
welcoming everyone
who came to visit you
the cousins and their wives
—their affection
your granddaughters
—Maïwenn to help after the fall
—Énora to gift you your ancestors' tree
your great grandson, Elvin
painting your nails
your great granddaughter, Morrigan
spontaneous and chatty
—I love you Mamichat she says
the train station in Nantes when they have to leave
the surrounding Garden of Plants with ponds and water birds
white magnolias lining the alleys
the screams and laughter around.

We will remember we were together
we will remember we were all alive.

Your last summer.

The Great Departure

September 20, 2024

You are no longer where you were, but you are everywhere that I am.
—Victor Hugo

Like you told me
every time I returned home
on the other side of the ocean,
"I'm going to miss you."

I will now hear you
in the light breeze.
I will look for you
in the flowers and the waves.
I will breathe your perfume
in the wild lavender fragrance.

*I would like to live until ninety-five,
it's a beautiful age,* you told me one day.
The orchid of your 95th birthday
withered the week of your death
after a rare four months bloom.

I will remember everything.
Your sky-blue raincoat in my childhood,
learning arithmetic in your jewelry store,
the hand knit turquoise mohair sweater,
your face living through the ages.

The recent moment when we watched
the equinox tide on Ré island,
wrapped up, our gaze lost.
Together.

Today your spirit has found its way
to the dear ones waiting for you:
your grand-mother Lechat, your sister Lili,
and your close friend John, who used to say:
*when two people are together and know
that the other loves them, joy is there.*

Yesterday
in the garden bowl
by your window
a robin came to drink.

Sixty-Five Years of Our Lives

*Where have they gone / the books read / the cities travelled /
by you / throughout your life?*
—Yvon Le Men

You lived for sixty-five years in this apartment,
on a wide avenue in the shadow of the Eiffel Tower,
views of a courtyard, maple trees and a school.
Plants and bird feeders on every window ledge.

In the shadow of the Eiffel Tower,
I went back through every room,
watering the plants on every window ledge,
looking for things to save from the clearing to come.

I went back through every room
looking for you, any sign, any message, any souvenir,
looking for things to save from the final clearing
—hand painted silk scarves, your owl collection, photo albums.

Looking for you, any sign, any message, any precious souvenir,
remembering my childhood and teenage years
captured in the photo albums
along with celebrations, travels and newborn babies.

Remembering my younger years
—you kept my letters, drawings and report cards
flipping through the celebrations and the travels,
unable to leave, I kept coming back for days on end.

I looked through my letters, drawings and report cards,
in sight of the courtyard, the maple trees and the school.
After coming back for days on end,
I reached peace with sixty-five years of our lives.

Haikoum for All Hallows Eve

October 31, 2024

The night when the veil thins
    —Robert Moss

It's All Hallows Eve.
The great Celtic festival,
Samhain, starts today.

The living, the dead,
the great Celtic festival
brings them together.

Samhain starts today.
A time to honor my dead,
our lives together.

Here comes All Saints' Day,
a time to honor my dead,
the end of harvest.

You loved All Saints' Day.
Earth is preparing to rest.
The end of harvest,

the start of autumn.
Earth is preparing to rest.
I'll adorn your tomb.

This start of autumn,
a pot of chrysanthemums
will adorn your tomb.

It's All Hallows Eve,
bright scarlet chrysanthemums
join living and dead.

Walking My Mother Home

You came in a dream last night . . .

A building full of people,
high white walls and corner shelves.
A hilly countryside, a stream below,
a pagoda and a cross in the garden.

I saw you, tiny but straight, on the rocky path
headed towards the bridge on the creek.
I joined you as we found our way
to your new room, spacious and quiet.

You had left keys behind in the old building.
As I was going to look for them, you said
*you don't have to come back yourself you know,
other people can bring them back.*

I woke up and I knew
that you're the one who won't come back,
but dreams are a treasure
where the lost ones return.

Mourning Doves

Hope is the thing with feathers.
—Emily Dickinson

In the old tree's core new life is coming.
A pair of mourning doves chose it for their nest.

> In the humble nest of twigs and grasses,
> I can see them a few feet away.

I contemplate them every morning
She is brooding, he is visiting.

> Hope and Espoir visiting me,
> as I named them.

Whispering their names, I sit and watch.
Am I wasting my time?

> Am I freeing my time?
> Mind blank, heart open.

In my heart a smile forms.
Is this a gift from you?

> Is this a message from you?
> You loved birds so much.

The birds that you loved
announce a new spring,

> an unstoppable spring.
> In my core joy is coming.

My Mother's Soup

I stay on the porch
until the orange gleams set behind
the naked cypresses and overgrown palms.

A few more minutes of light each day
prepare me for the first spring of her absence.

The owls hoot softly in the depth of the trees.
On my desk, my mother's carved wooden owl
watches over me peacefully.

The blue hydrangeas defy the winter cold.
The blue jays call into the twilight.
There are days that we live as if death was nowhere.[7]

When it's dark, I go back inside
to prepare the soup I grew up on.

---

[7] Li Young Lee

Enchanted Episode

A summer holiday village,
wooden chalets among the pine trees,
the families of resident cats,
the miles long beach.

The Reef Bar right on the sand,
old anchors and a compass on the walls,
a terrace overlooking the horizon.
A coffee, a glass of water, a notebook, a pen,
the hidden harmony of things.

Memories of my mother last time we were here,
her absence like a silent ache,
the silver blue balm of the ocean at dusk,
the plans for tomorrow.

The joy of a little boy,
his request to mark the map
with all the things we've done
—restaurant, merry go round, guided tour

"For when we come back" he says.

Your Special Day

Often, I asked what you would like
for your birthday.
In your younger years,
we would go shop together
—a pure wool cardigan, a silk blouse.

As the years went by,
you would say "I have everything."
I tried to surprise you with small gifts
—a gourmet dinner, red roses sent from abroad.

For your sixtieth birthday in the Meudon garden
—a thick shearling coat.

When you turned seventy
—a trip to the Niagara Falls.

When you turned eighty in joyful Provence,
—a new computer, faster and more readable.

At ninety, four generations together
wrote a song for you to the tune of
La Ballade des Gens Heureux.[8]

---

[8] *The Ballad of Happy People*

For your last birthday, the ninety-fifth in Brittany,
—a reclining armchair, a radiant orchid.

May is a month of spring and hope,
the 16th will always be your day.

So, what would you like,
for your birthday this year?

Aftersense

A hibiscus bouquet
next to a collage of your pictures,
can you see them?

Your fuchsia silk scarf,
soft and warm around my neck,
can you feel it?

A rose scented candle,
your favorite subtle fragrance,
can you smell it?

The songs that you played,
their melodies fill the sky,
can you hear them?

The champagne you liked,
effervescent bubbles of joy,
can you taste them?

All Will Be Said

It will be spring,
already six months since you left.
Swallows will have returned.

I will drive alone
to the place where you were born,
singing your preferred psalm.

*In the green grass fields,
I rest. Nothing is missing.
I have no fear.*

Where the village ends,
in the quiet cemetery,
you and I will meet.

I will be silent,
and in that silence,
all will be said.

You may give me a sign
—a dove, a rainbow, a butterfly
that I will cherish.

Living so far away,
I will bring ceramic roses
that never die.

Heritage

Things you left me

The white sofa set, a key piece of my "French corner"
along with the mahogany game table made by your grandfather,
hand covered pillows we created for my student room.

Coffee table books of Monet paintings,
old books of poetry by Victor Hugo,
illustrated books with Japanese gardens.

Shiny wooden trays, carmine red bowls, eggshell candle holders
with over ten layers of tree sap lacquer,
years of birthday gifts.

The gold semainier[9] bracelet made of seven thin bands,
the gold shells necklace gifted for my departure from France,
the gold pendant I had made with your fingerprint.

The panoramic postcard of Paris when I left
think of Paris sometimes, you wrote.
the WhatsApp chats, the big news, the little news.

---

[9] A French term for a type of bracelet made of seven bands, one for each day of the week

Pictures in your 40s, 60s, 80s,
watching the sea, holding babies, holding cats,
enjoying a glass of port, smiling for eternity.

The letter you wrote before surgery a few years ago
discovered in the bottom of a drawer
Je ne regrette ni d'être venue,
ni de devoir repartir vers l'inconnu.[10]

---

[10] *I have no regrets about having been here, or about having to leave for the unknown.*

About the Author

Anne-Marie Derouault writes free verse poetry in English and in French, haikus and short stories, inspired by her love of travel, nature, and human beings.

She was born in Paris, France, and has resided in Florida for many years. Her first poetry book was a bilingual collection, *While the Poem Lasts / Le Temps d'un Poème* (2018), which was featured in a video interview with *bUneke Magazine*. Her writings have appeared in the Brevard Scribblers anthology series *Written in the Sun;* the Space Coast Writers Guild Anthologies *Survival, Horizons, and Transformations;* and Precious Publishing's *Pandemic*.

Previous endeavors include being an executive in the computer industry with a Ph.D. in Computational Linguistics from Paris University and a degree in Psychology. She later founded Emergence Resources, LLC, to offer training and coaching internationally on communication and stress reduction.

In addition to extensive traveling in Europe and Asia, she has had a lifelong passion for yoga and mindfulness, and is a registered teacher with the USA Yoga Alliance. She created two Relaxation CDs, "Letting Go" and "Harmony with Food", and self-published a series of Mindful Eating Handbooks.

She continues to spend a couple of months a year visiting the old continent to renew her inspiration and nurture her relationships. She currently lives on the Space Coast of Florida, never far from the ocean, on a land where opossums, bobcats, hawks and doves live and play.

www.ingramcontent.com/pod-product-compliance
Lightning Source LLC
Chambersburg PA
CBHW022015160426
43197CB00007B/438